Copyright © 2020 Empower Your Life LLC

All Rights Reserved. No part of this publication may be reproduced or transmitted in any form or by any means, mechanical or electronic, including photocopying and recording, or by any information storage and retrieval system, without permission in writing from the author or publisher (except by a reviewer, who may quote brief passages and/or show brief video clips in a review).

Disclaimer: The Publisher and the Author make no representation or warranties concerning the accuracy or completeness of the contents of this work and specifically disclaim all warranties for a particular purpose. No warranty may be created or extended through sales or promotional materials. The advice and strategies contained herein may not be suitable for every situation. This work is sold with the understanding that the Author and Publisher are not engaged in rendering legal, technological, or other professional services. If professional assistance is required, the services of a competent professional should be sought. Neither the Publisher nor the Author shall be liable for damages arising therefrom.

The fact that an organization or website is referred to in this work as a citation and/or potential source of further information does not mean that the Author or the Publisher endorses the information, the organization, or website it may provide or recommendations it may make. Further, readers should be aware that websites listed in this work may have changed or disappeared between when this work was written and when it is read.

Disclaimer: The cases and stories in this book have had details changed to preserve privacy.

Getting Out Alive: ISBN: Paperback 9781648731150 ISBN: EBOOK 9781648731112 **Survivor Basics:** ISBN: EBOOK 9781648731136 ISBN: Paperback 9781648731167 **Initial Beginnings:** ISBN: Paperback 9781648731174 ISBN: EBOOK 9781648731129 **12 Step Guide to Restoration:** ISBN: Paperback 9781648731181 ISBN: EBOOK 9781648731143

Printed in the United States of America

Published by:
Writer's Publishing House
Prescott, Az 86301

Cover and Interior Design by Creative Artistic Excellence Marketing
Project Management and Book Launch by Creative Artistic Excellence Marketing
https://lizzymcnett.com

**National Domestic
Abuse Hotline
1-800-799-7233**

12- Step Restoration Program

Survivor Basics

By Purposed Survivor

Table of Contents

Table of Contents _____ 4

Introduction _____ 8

Chapter One:

In What Way It Works _____ 10

Chapter Two

Why Are We Here? _____ 17

Chapter Three

What is Restoration? _____ 19

Chapter Four:

Education vs Intelligence _____ 23

Mind Power One - Strength: _____ 34

"The word "strength" means "to endure," "to persist." Strength is the ability to keep on keeping on, despite negative conditions in a person's body or affairs." _____ 34

Mind Power Two - Faith: _____ 45

"What you are firm about in your thinking, you are firm about in your faith." _____ 45

Mind Power Three Judgement: _____ 52
> "The ability to understand our life and the choices we made." _____ 52

Mind Power Four Love: _____ 61
> "Just as the heart equalizes the flow in the body, so love harmonizes the thoughts of the mind, bringing peace to both mind and body." _____ 61
> An Inventory of Ourselves _____ 63
> Abuse _____ 68
> Assets _____ 69

Mind Power Five Power: _____ 73
> "Every word brings forth after its kind - first in mind, then in body, and eventually the affairs of the individual." _____ 73

Mind Power Six Imagination: _____ 78
> "The imagination is the scissors of the mind; you create the pictures, which take your thoughts and give them form." _____ 78
> Vision _____ 80
> The List _____ 83

Mind Power Seven Understanding: _____ 86
> "Understanding: Realizing past experiences can only harm my future when they are left unattended." ___ 86
> Taking Action _____ 89

Mind Power Eight Will: 91
"Depend on the power of belief." _____ 91
Forgiveness Letters _____ 93

Mind Power Nine Order: 97
"Discern the difference between _____ 97
acknowledgment and acceptance." _____ 97
Making Amends _____ 102

Mind Power Ten Zeal: 104
"A graceful, flexible attitude working within each person, manifesting as great compassion and love." _____ 104
Feeling Versus Action _____ 105
Taking My First Personal Inventory _____ 109

Mind Power Eleven Elimination: 111
"The power of elimination is constantly infusing more energy into one's being, and simultaneously casting out of mind and body all waste. The forgiving love of our Higher Power is not only a wonderful spiritual stimulation for the soul and body, it is an important factor in the elimination process. It causes an infusion of the new as letting go of the old takes place." _____ 111
Praying and Meditation _____ 112

Chapter Six:

Confidence for Life _____ **117**

Mind Power Twelve Life: _____ 126

"To affirm 'life' will make the life force flow throughout the body." _____ 126

Practicing These Principles Daily _____ 129

Setting Boundaries_____ 131

Introduction

Welcome to the Purposed Survivor 12 Phases to Restoration. The Initial Beginnings book is a discussion of the *12 Phases*. We all came into this seeking restoration from an abusive situation. In this case, we understand the commonalities of each person's accounts, but written or verbal, no one individual's restoration is the same. This book is not meant to be an exhaustive study, nor is it meant to be the final work on any aspect of restoration. Rather, it is meant to help determine your interpretation of the principles contained in our steps and traditions. Our hope is that you will find peace from the restoration process. We pray you will find a complete guide to living without existing in the ramifications of domestic abuse.

We collectively pray this book brings a valued therapeutic massage to your restoration program. It is through one survivor helping another that we find restoration, a connection with our Higher Power and the message of hope for the future.

Chapter One:

In What Way It Works

"What you get by achieving your goals is not as important as what you become by achieving your goals." Henry David Thoreau

The information in Survivor Basics is based on individual accounts of others who have overcome the debilitating effects of domestic abuse. We bring restoration to our own lives when we share the message of hope to others.

    The chapters in this book are written to help Purposed Survivors in the process of restoration. While Purposed Survivor was designed to inspire anyone who seeks restoration, ultimately the choice falls upon each person to pursue success. However, these words are only meant as a guide, not the final word on the restoration process.

    On this day:

"I will take an inventory of the achievements in my life, taking care not to disregard any accomplishments, no matter how small, remembering success can only be achieved with consistency."

It is with gratitude in our restoration, we acknowledge the continued development of our conscious contact with God that no survivor seeking freedom from abuse ever be denied a better way to live.

We remain trusted servants to our Higher Power

"If you make my word your home, you will indeed be my protectants. You will know the truth and the truth will set you free."

We welcome you to read the text written in this book. It is with hope that you find a path to freedom and restoration. However, change will only come when you make the initial step.

Purposed Survivor was founded on achieving a life without abuse. It is through a greater consciousness that guided our direction and enabled us to build on a proven program to further the goal of eliminating a life of abuse for anyone seeking freedom.

Purposed Survivors come from all walks of life…. but we have one common denominator, a solution for our abusive situation. Our goal is that any survivor seeking freedom may find a solution that works for them.

Purposed Survivor is not a religious program, but is based on a set of spiritual principles guided by a God of your Understanding.

Consider this prayer as you begin this journey.

"God, we pray that your will guide all our endeavors and your will alone. We are servants to the God of our Understanding, and through our acknowledgement of the spiritual principles, may our conscious contact be strengthened. We pray that no Purposed Survivor need suffer from abuse when they seek freedom."

To be fully connected with a God of our understanding, it's imperative to activate our twelve mind powers. As you progress in this book, each mind power will be explained throughout the twelve sections. Below is a complete list of all twelve powers and where they are located in the body.

- Strength- Small of the back (behind the adrenal glands)
- Faith – Center brain (pineal gland)
- Judgment – Solar plexus (pit of the stomach)
- Love – Back of the heart (near the thymus gland)
- Power – Root of the tongue (near the thyroid gland)
- Imagination – Between the eyes (near the pituitary gland)
- Understanding – Forehead above eyes (front brain)
- Will – Forehead (center of the front brain)
- Order – Behind the naval (large nerve center behind the naval), a subconscious area of the body to expel emotions first.
- Zeal – Back of the neck (base of the brain)
- Elimination – Lower back (organs of elimination)

- Life – Generative organs

Who is a Purposed Survivor?

"Some of us wondered if there was hope of getting out alive, or how we would ever succeed in this quest. The answer is yes, getting out alive is possible, and we can live a life free from abuse."

If you have found Purposed Survivor, there is no need to ask if you have suffered from an abusive situation. Most of us already know the answer.

The type of abuse does not matter. Some people think only physical abuse causes a problem. However, this is not the case. Mental abuse may not leave bumps and bruises, but the scars last a lifetime. Either way, one or both reasons have led you to this program.

None of us ever wanted to be put in harm's way by someone we thought loved us. The idea was never an image of personal freedom or personal commitment. It was something that just happened, and by the time we realized the true nature of the relationship, our survival was in jeopardy. We began to convince ourselves that everything would be alright, and then the 'IF's took place. Instead of admitting the true nature of the abusive situation, we chose to make excuses for why the abuse took place. Denial comes in many forms, and none of the excuses are valid. Abuse is never acceptable for any reason.....

The relationship eventually incarcerated us as prisoners to our abuser, without any chance of parole. At some point, before coming to Purposed Survivor, we decided to surrender to the hopelessness of our situation and ask for help. We then committed to seek restoration in our lives and live free from abuse. It was only after this choice that our hope for restoration became a reality. The horrors of our abuse will always be part of the past and memories, but we can learn to give up the continued torment.

By committing to our restoration, we can progress and eventually help other survivors. At this point, we can accept the abuse as a purpose to help advance our greater good..... eventually, assisting others to do the same.

When we entered the abusive situation, we had no inkling of what the future may hold or the abuse we would face. We acted on feelings and emotions instead of knowledge and experience. Some of us were acting on learned behavior, while others fell into the hidden agenda of others. Or, our paths intersected with the same result. Through these lines, we found Purposed Survivor, and our lives were forever changed again. In the process of seeking our restoration, we came to the understanding that only when we truly commit to the spiritual principles can our lives become manageable.

Chapter Two

Why Are We Here?

As Purposed Survivors, we sought a new way of life. Our past is trauma, pain, guilt, hopelessness, anger, and lack. We survived in deplorable conditions, functioned under extreme stress, and feared our life was threatened daily. The relationship caused us to cry tears of compassion for our families, choked down anger for the uncontrollable situation, and sought refuge continually.

> 'For the tree can be told by its fruit. You brood of vipers, how can your speech be honest, when you are evil? For words flow out of what fills the heart. Good people draw worthwhile things from their store of goodness; bad people draw unpleasant things from their store of badness. So, I tell you for every false word people utter they will answer on Judgment Day since your words will justify and condemn you.'

All these conditions brought us to the conclusion that our existence depended on finding a new way of life. The fear of residing in our current situation overpowered the fear of remaining one minute longer. Our patterns are learned behavior, either from family history teaching, or we sought refuge from fear of being alone. In either case, we chose to escape the abuse with an idea that hope could give us freedom.

When we finally became a Purposed Survivor, the concept of hope came alive for us, and we could visualize a future without abuse.

Chapter Three

What is Restoration?

The purpose of restoration is simply living free from the ramifications of domestic abuse. If you are willing to make an effort to find the solution to freedom, then these are the basic steps you must take to find freedom.

- We admitted we were powerless to our abuser- and the life we lived was unmanageable.
- We came to believe that a power greater than ourselves could restore us to sanity.
- We decided to trust the God of our understanding and then turn our will and our lives over to him.
- We made a searching and fearless moral inventory of ourselves.
- We admitted to God, to ourselves, and to another human being the embarrassment and humiliation of our acceptance of the violence that retained our life.

- We were entirely ready to release and ask God to remove all of these imperfections of character.
- We humbly asked Him to remove our shortcomings.
- We made a list of all persons who harmed us, and became willing to make peace with our abusers and accept judgment is bestowed only by the god of our understanding.
- We made direct amends to ourselves and forgiveness statements to the people who have injured us.
- We continue to seek restoration through a daily personal inventory and accept responsibility for our actions.

Through prayer and meditation, we sought to improve our conscious contact with God as we understood Him.

In this process, we may encounter a spiritual awakening... one that will change the course of our lives forever.

Planning a life free from abuse is not something anyone should consider. Abuse of any kind is unacceptable. However, there are some questions you may want to ask yourself.

- Do you want to leave your abusive situation?
- Are you prepared for the difficulties of leaving?
- Have you accepted the abusive relationship and understand it's an unnatural way of life?
- Do you fully comprehend the results if you stay?
- Do injuries, violence, or even the fear of death plague your thoughts daily?
- Do you acknowledge the abusive situation changed you into someone you don't want to be?
- Do you participate in things because of physical force or threats?
- Do you believe you are a failure and the abusive situation controls every aspect of your life?

If you answer yes to any of these questions, then you have picked up the right book to read. Our fear of failure can eliminate any possibility of success if we let that frame of mind control our thoughts. It is never too late to admit you made a mistake and want to proceed with a better way of life. However, this decision takes determination to pursue a life filled with personal choices, ones that are not forced upon us by someone else. Only after we have made the conscious choice to escape our situation, can we truly find the freedom we seek? Any doubt can create an opening for excuses and denying the reality of your relationship. When you finally choose to craft an opening for the life you desire, commit to achieving restoration on the merit of terms you set for yourself, not for someone else.

Chapter Four:

Education vs Intelligence

Have you ever thought about the difference between Education and Intelligence? There is a vast difference between the two. However, there is one connection, they both involve knowledge. Otherwise, they are unique concepts.

Webster's dictionary states intelligence is the ability to learn, try, or understand new situations, vs. Education, which defines it as the field of study that deals with methods of teaching or learning in a particular subject. In this case, intelligence is an innate ability, and education is a learned habit. , and naturalist.

Intelligence naturally varies in degrees and can be developed through education and training. Therefore, intelligence must be an internal force that controls our ability to get distinct skill sets.

Education is something provided through an external system, normally from a mentor, teacher, or parent. Our edification builds your natural abilities. In other words, people vary in innate skills and will naturally shine when fulfilling their latent talents. The possibilities are endless when you consider this additional information about intelligence vs. education. However, with every new theory comes criticism. Some psychologists and educators think the idea of trying to define intelligence is too broad. They simply believe those traits are talents, personality traits, and abilities. Nevertheless, many teachers have capitalized on the theory and started using the idea in their classrooms.

      Educators believe that once you learn more about multiple intelligences, it can help develop your strengths. Continue reading to learn more about the major characteristics of each type of intelligence. If you still aren't sure which type describes you best, this quiz can help you figure it out.

Visual-Spatial Intelligence

Strengths: Visual and spatial judgment

- Are you good at visualizing things?
- Typically, these people are good at directions, reading maps, charts, videos, or pictures?

Major Characters

- Enjoys reading and writing
- Good at putting puzzles together
- Good at interpreting pictures, graphs, and charts
- Enjoys drawing, painting, and the visual arts
- Recognizes patterns easily
- Career Options
- Architect
- Artist
- Engineer

Strengths: Words, language, and writing

Are you good at verbal communication, able to recognize words well both written and spoken? Typically, these people can tell stories, memorize information, and read.

Major Characteristics

- Enjoys reading and writing
- Good at putting puzzles together
- Good at interpreting pictures, graphs, and charts
- Enjoys drawing, painting, and the visual arts
- Recognizes patterns easily
- Career Options
- Writer/journalist
- Lawyer
- Teacher
- Logical-Mathematical Intelligence

Strengths: Analyzing problems and mathematical operations

Are you good at mathematical problems? Typically, these people are adept at reasoning, problem-solving, patterns. Generally, numbers, analyzing, and relationships.

- Major Characteristics
- Excellent problem-solving skills
- Enjoys thinking about abstract ideas

- Likes conducting scientific experiments
- Good at solving complex computations
- Career Options
- Scientist
- Mathematician
- Computer programmer
- Engineer
- Accountant

Bodily-Kinesthetic Intelligence

Strengths: Physical movement, motor control

Are you good at body movement, performing actions, and physical control? Typically, these people have excellent eye-hand coordination and dexterity.

Major Characteristics

- Good at dancing and sports
- Enjoys creating things with his or her hands
- Excellent physical coordination
- Tends to remember by doing, rather than hearing or seeing

Career Options

- Dancer
- Builder
- Sculptor
- Actor

Musical Intelligence

Strengths: Rhythm and music

Are you good at thinking in patterns, rhythms, sounds? Typically, these people appreciate music, and often compose songs, or perform musically.

Major Characteristics

- Enjoys singing and playing musical instruments
- Recognizes musical patterns and tones easily
- Good at remembering songs and melodies
- A rich understanding of musical structure, rhythm, and notes

Career Options

- Musician
- Composer
- Singer
- Music teacher
- Conductor

Interpersonal Intelligence

Strengths: Understanding and relating to other people

Are you good at understanding people and communicating? Typically, these people are good at evaluating emotions, motivations, desires, and intentions of individuals around them.

Major Characteristics

- Characteristics of interpersonal intelligence include:
- Good at communicating verbally
- Skilled at nonverbal communication
- Sees situations from different perspectives
- Creates positive relationships with others
- Good at resolving conflict in groups

Career Options

If you're strong in interpersonal intelligence, good career choices for you are:

- Psychologist
- Philosopher
- Counselor
- Salesperson
- Politician

- Intrapersonal Intelligence

Strengths: Introspection and self-reflection

Are you good at being aware of emotional states, enjoy self-reflection, exploring relationships? Typically, these people are good at assessing their strengths.

Major Characteristics

- Good at analyzing his or her strengths and weaknesses
- Enjoys analyzing theories and ideas
- Excellent self-awareness
- Clearly understands the basis for his or her motivations and feelings

Career Options

- Philosopher
- Writer
- Theorist
- Scientist

Naturalistic Intelligence

Strengths: Finding patterns and relationships to nature

Are you good at nurturing the environment by learning about other species? Typically, these people are good at understanding subtle changes in their environment.

Major Characteristics

- Interested in subjects such as botany, biology, and zoology
- Good at categorizing and cataloging information easily
- May enjoy camping, gardening, hiking, and exploring the outdoors
- Doesn't enjoy learning unfamiliar topics that have no connection to nature

Career Options

- Biologist
- Conservationist
- Gardener
- Farmer

At this point, no definitive theory exists on the true nature of intelligence or how education plays into the scheme of things, but one thing is for sure. The only way to understand your inner abilities is to explore all possibilities. Learn your likes and dislikes, then expand on their potential.

Mind Power One - Strength:

"The word "strength" means "to endure," "to persist." Strength is the ability to keep on keeping on, despite negative conditions in a person's body or affairs."

Upon first glance of the past, we may view it as failure, and success or survival are hidden from sight. The fear, worry, and anguish had taken over every thought process we had. It's only at this time that we can truly see the light of day. Our past and present must meet in the middle, so to speak, for clarity.

Only after we recognize the reality of our situation, can we acknowledge the outcome of our current way of life. To continue in this fashion, there can only be an ending of sadness or death. Therefore, we must find the strength to leave. This is a point in our life, however, in which the highest danger resides. But we must acknowledge the only way to find restoration is to leave.

Preparing for departure is not always an option, sometimes it occurs on the spur of the moment, and we reside only on instinct to guide us to safety. It's after departure, and reality of our situation becomes clear that we begin to construct thoughts about why we should return. At these times, we must cease any immediate action and remain calm, never lose faith in our decision.

In this phase, we learn the true meaning of strength, endurance, and persistence. There is an old Italian proverb that says, "He conquers who endures." Ancient philosophers taught the way to eliminate evil from one's world, and body was to perpetually declare, "there is no strength or power but in God the good."

Strength is more than just a physical characteristic, it's a state of mind in both health and conscious thought. People who suffer from many ailments are not always organically sick; their lack of strength comes from mental, emotional, or spiritual weakness.

By working through this phase, we find the solution to where strength comes from and how we endured such turmoil. It's only after working through these phases that we understand the nature of our existence. We begin acknowledging that the problems were not always of our own doing, nor were we to blame for the abuse.

Phase One provides us with the strength to admit our powerlessness. However, admission is not enough. We must truly accept the situation for what it was, no one can ever hope for a better past. The past is ours, no matter the circumstances. Our decision can never be changed. Therefore, it is time determine the patterns of behavior that caused us to make these decisions. In doing so, we establish a clear map of the past, bringing into focus the real problems behind our abusive situation. The clarity will allow us to move forward with an understanding of our actions in the future.

Often, we avoid the truth because it causes us pain or shame. When we deny the actions of our abuser, the strength we have gained is lost again. Acceptance is part of restoration.

The definition of denial is "a refusal to believe in something or admit that something exists."

Our denial is valid but causes lack of acceptance. To admit powerlessness over any situation is complicated, even unnerving at times. Nevertheless, we can only hope for restoration when we surrender and trust in the God of our understanding. His guidance can relieve any discomfort we may be feeling.

When we find ourselves in situations that are out of our control, and there is no room for an escape without injury, the time has come for change. No relationship should ever be open to abuse of any kind, mental or physical.

At one point, if you look closely at your situation, there were signs that most of us did not want to see, let alone feel. These clues gave the insight we needed to face the abuse, either before or right after it started. We are all looking for love and a solid family foundation; one in which we can be safe and find security. It was for these reasons we stayed when our heart told us to leave. As time progressed and the situation got worse, we began denying the abuse and violent behavior. The reality of the circumstances became too much to bear. Our minds, feelings, and spirit died inside. We barely existed…

We went from being someone who loved life and wanted the best for ourselves and family to someone we could not even recognize in the mirror.

The bitterness of letting the abuse continue directed toward our abuser and ourself slowly kills any hope of having a bright future. So, we tried to avoid contact with anyone, except those encounters we could not avoid. Our feelings were kept hidden. It was the only way we could protect what little dignity we had left. Shielding our innermost emotions helped us maintain power in our helpless situation. It was this undying devotion to survival that got us out of our abusive situation.

Another ugly facet of abuse is manageability in our life. We can only conquer what we accept and surrender to the reality of the violence. Most of us knew deep down the seriousness of our abusive relationship but kept insisting things would change. All we had to do was correct problems with money, sex, family, or career. However, as we worked on fixing one area, another would fall apart.

The more we worked on trying to fix all the problems at any cost, the abuse continued to rage out of control. We became obsessed with solving the problems, while we continued to die inside. The actions of someone else cannot be changed. Instead, turn to prayer for their well-being; release them in love with their higher good. However, each person is responsible for their actions. When we try to change someone or something, we lose sight of what and who we are. As abuse victims, we have a built-in compulsion to create resolutions for any problem, especially when it is regarding someone we love or care about. Our fear of confrontation is the direct result of this compulsion. Whether the fear started as a young child reared in a violent situation, or from an experience later in life, does not matter. The reservation must be acknowledged to release the feeling and move forward with our restoration. Until we can surrender to the fear and release its hold over our minds, the unmanageability will continue.

In any situation, we can find ourselves hesitant or unsure. These emotions are healthy and required for survival. It is only when we ignore these feelings that trouble occurs. We must recognize these reservations and acknowledge their existence. By admitting the apprehensions, we can restore our lives. Our feelings keep us aware of the past, a reminder of the abuse without hindering our healing process. These emotions will excel in the process because we confess our shame and embarrassment.

There is no worse feeling than having to admit the shame, embarrassment, and fear of our relationship. The full magnitude of our situation was beginning to set in, and the fear of failure was high. The exposure left us feeling naked and alone. Our minds raced with thoughts of what-ifs, and how can I? It is true that facing the world alone, without the security of the abusive situation is terrifying. Even though we knew the risks of remaining with our abuser, it was familiar and the only stability in our lives at the time. Our only thoughts were how to fix the problem... make everything the way we dreamed it should be. The fear told us that we could manipulate the abuser and make them realize their wrongs. However, we could only see the consequences that caused the problems, not the solution. In this decision, the solution came to us because we chose freedom.

Surrender is a powerful word and can greatly enhance our lives when we fully grasp the meaning. Strength comes from surrendering to the acceptance of our abusive relationship(s). The one mistake you don't want to make is simply resigning to the abuse; in this case, you are not truly accepting the experience. Only when you can surrender and be at peace with the life you have lived can restoration begin.

Have you heard of the saying; time heals all wounds? In some cases, this may be true, but not when it comes to abuse, both mental and physical. There will always be damage that you do not fully comprehend. Certain situations will occur, and you may experience an unanticipated reaction. For example, the deep stern tone of a man's voice, the pop of an aluminum can being opened, quarrelsome situations with family, friends, strangers, or even the simple act of having someone sternly tell you what needs to be done. These are merely a few situations, so you must be fully aware of the manifested effects abuse has had on your psyche. As stated above, you will never fully recover from the abuse, but you can find restoration and live a complete and happy life again.

The healing process is unique to each person, and it's yours to feel. As you begin to understand and surrender to the abusive relationship, unexpected emotions may cause extreme waves of uncertainty or confusion. At this point, render the feelings, search them out, and most of all, feel them. Keep an open mind and explore the possibilities for restoration from these experiences. It will make you stronger....

Strong feelings are part of the aftershock of abuse. It's normal to have emotional mood swings and uncontrolled outbursts from time to time. The mind, body, and soul are in a state of repair and healing. Embrace the emotions, and accept the healing process.

The principal factor of this phase is to acknowledge the powerlessness to your abuser. To accomplish surrender, you must keep an open mind and accept the abuse as part of your past; be ready to move forward with your restoration. Therefore, identifying that you're human and things happen sometimes at no fault of your own is a crucial part of healing. It's not where you were that matters; it's where you are going.

We must do more than simply accept the abuse in our past to continue with a positive and successful future. The search begins with an inventory of the things that are hurting or angering us the most and then accepting those things for what they are. The next phase is finding an organization with people who understand the trauma you endured and are willing to help discover your dynamic natural abilities.

As you come to the end of this phase, you may wonder, how did I possibly make it this far? The answer is strength. To evoke the power of your mind and body takes one simple thing: the elimination of doubt. Putting your faith in a Higher Power not only guides you to success but builds a strong mental character to withstand future situations.

To discover how we can survive a life without abuse, we must first understand the cause. Then we have to acknowledge the choices we made that led to the abusive situation. Remember, nothing changes if nothing changes.

Mind Power Two - Faith:

"What you are firm about in your thinking, you are firm about in your faith."

William James described the power of faith as not only believing in a higher power but also power for your health. He said, "Faith is the habitual center of man's energies."

One of the first things you must do to restore health is to believe in a Higher Power greater than yourself. Sometimes when life steers us in directions away from a conscious contact with God, so we lose the ability to communicate regularly with Him. At this time, our lives become unmanageable.

If you are reading and starting to work through these phases it is because the life you have been living is not working. Avoiding any options that might say otherwise is denial in all its glory. We learn that faith is working all the time, no matter what is happening in your life. Your faith is the direct result of what you pay the most attention. Therefore, it is imperative to focus on what's good in your life and continue to manifest the best possible outcome for the future.

The following chapter is about faith and coming to believe in a power greater than yourself. Relinquishing any doubt or misgivings about what faith is or is not must be the first action. Starting this phase with a clear head, void of all preconceptions will allow your faith to grow in miraculous ways you cannot even imagine. Faith is probably one of the most powerful words in the English language. Simply saying the word, one can create incredible results immediately. Of all the 12 mind powers, faith is the only mind power that can overcome any circumstance in your life at this time. The first goal will be to understand the barriers you may face. The second is learning to identify what faith means.

By accepting abuse as a normal part of life, we acknowledge the lack of faith in ourselves. Accepting the past brings us to a new way of thinking. Once we acknowledge the abuse, it becomes part of our conscious thoughts. Awareness is necessary for healing our mind, body, and spirit.

The concept of hope has driven mankind for generations. It is the binding force behind our survival, the endurance to continue when all seems lost and no end is in sight. It gives us renewed optimism each morning.

When we chose this path, the idea of a better life did not seem possible, but HOPE is why we opened this book. Our renewed optimism came when we realized other people, just like ourselves, have progressed with purpose. Their lives are now based on meaning, not fear, and abuse.

You may not recognize the hope for success at this point, but by acknowledging the abuse, your pain is accompanied by a surge of hope, making it possible to continue with the next phase of your life.

1. What do I have hope for today?

The question of unmanageability in our life was never doubted. The problem became, how do I stop it or get out alive? Many times, we are told "just walk away," or "why did you get involved in the first place?"

In most cases, if we had that answer, we'd probably not be walking in these shoes. Our insanity is why we continued to remain as long as we did.

The dictionary defines insanity as, "a lack of reason or good sense, extreme foolishness or an act that demonstrates such foolishness."

There are no simple solutions to the problem. All we can do is continue to work on ourselves. By understanding behavior and the reasons we made these choices, we should be able to avoid the same violent relationships, which is the true meaning of insanity.

1. The question you need to ask is, how insane was the true nature of your abusive relationship?

What some of us consider insane is a normal way of life for someone else, therefore it's imperative we do not judge another person's choices. We must accept them for who they are and love them regardless of the decisions they make.

Insanity is a loss of perspective or a sense of proportion. In other words, our lives are out of balance. Gaining perspective on any situation requires constant inspection of our daily activities.

1. What do we place as important or priorities in our life?

Each point has its meaning, you just have to decide which is most important, and remain vigilant in acting appropriately.

We can always choose a better way of life when we fill ourselves with love, compassion, trust, and hope. The conscious contact you can develop with your Higher Power gives these things free of charge. You just have to be willing to accept them.

The word *restoration* is defined as "the return of something removed or abolished."

In this situation, the restoration is you, the elimination of trying to be something you are not for the sake of someone else's misguided needs. For your healing and spiritual growth, you must have a firm grasp on the meaning of insanity. This includes the continuation of irrational behavior.

Sometimes, the changes in our lives are gradual, and we may even wonder if all this work is worth the effort. But as time passes and our restoration is progressing, we will sometimes get impatient or restless, wanting an immediate fix to all the problems. This, however, is impossible. Restoration is a gradual process and requires dedication. On the other hand, once you recognize unrealistic behavior in your life, it's a good sign. You are finally beginning to understand the meaning of insanity.

One sign that faith has settled in our lives, is the ability to make decisions with careful deliberation. We stop making rash and spur-of-the-moment choices. Once the clarity of peace becomes a daily routine, our need for further restoration is welcome. The favor of greater good is establishing itself in your everyday routine.

The concept of restoration and living a life without abuse may seem foreign at this point, even impossible. However, it does not matter if you understand the power of God; the important factor is you believe restoration is possible. Faith will be the guide.

As you come to the end of Phase Two, understand that each phase of the process has its lessons, and not all information will be revealed at once. Don't be discouraged if your progress is slower than you anticipated or not what you expected. The acknowledgment of faith is different for each person, and so is the restoration. Be patient, all will be revealed when the time is appropriate.

Mind Power Three
Judgement:

"The ability to understand our life and the choices we made."

The mind power of judgment is located in the stomach, which is the substance center of the body. Your stomach nourishes your body, just like your mind nourishes the soul. If you feed your mind with negative thoughts and malnourish your body, each center will act accordingly. There is no difference between the information, either good or bad.

Therefore, keeping a positive attitude will nourish your mind and body with a life-giving substance.

Phase Three is what centers the mind and body to one frame of thought: the idea of surrender. You can accomplish almost anything when you surrender to the will of your Higher Power and release all past hurts, pain, and abuse. Remember, you cannot change the past, only learn from it and move forward with an open heart. The willingness to educate yourself on positive outcomes is a personal choice.

This process comes from time and patience, but not without work on your part. Restoration comes with the price of exercising sound mental practices. Working through these phases with an open mind and willingness to learn is one of the only obligations required for success. Your achievements rest solely on the motivation to change your life. The doubts and fears carried inside will only minimize your restoration.

We may find ourselves filled with the memories of our abusive relationship and afraid to commit to restoration because a fear of failure. This time, however, is unique in the sense that the decision to make this change is of your own doing. No one is forcing or controlling us to do something against our will. This one simple choice creates the movement for success. When we finally realize that freedom is possible and we can live free from abuse, our eyes are open, so we can begin to understand how wonderful life can be.

Most of us came into this program believing that another human being was responsible for our happiness.

- We had spent much of our time trying to please them at all costs when the effort was futile. Our first reaction was to torment ourselves with guilt, fear, and worry.
- We'd then spent countless hours trying to figure out what we could do differently next time, and all the while our abuser manipulated the situation as they saw fit.
- Our abusers' emotions ranged from rage to tenderness. They became tornadoes whipping through the lives of everyone in sight, completely unconscious of the path of destruction they left behind. If circumstances

were not to their liking, they would seek any means necessary to achieve their wants and get their way, no matter the cost.
- Each of them was so aimed at aggressively pursuing their impulses, any conscious thought was nonexistent. This usually meant an explosive incidence, with personal injuries and sometimes death.

The content of this paragraph may be graphic, but reality can be harsh. To accept the past for what it is, the truth must be revealed.

The actions necessary to reveal the truth of our situation are something we must willingly acknowledge and work surrendering to the past hurts. In doing so, we concede our self-will. The mind is a powerful force, and when left to work independently from the rest of our mental powers, it quickly takes control of every aspect of our lives. Self-will is a trait all humans have, and when exercised accordingly, it can be a positive thing in our lives.

Will is the focal point around which all mind action centers when the mind is harmonious. The twin mind powers are will and understanding. They work together, but only when we keep a close reign on our *will*. The struggle to override our mind power of understanding is strong and can be difficult to control when not exercised regularly. This is a practice that takes time to accomplish.

The dictionary states that *will* "is the part of the mind with which somebody consciously decides things, the power to make decisions, the determination to do something."

It also states *will* "is the attitude or feelings somebody has toward somebody or something."

These definitions have powerful meanings, and their explanations should not be taken lightly. Focus and clarity are the keys to understanding your *will* and God's *will*.

As you progress, the principles are invaluable to everyday experiences. They will give you the foundation necessary to achieve the goals you have set for your life.

There are a few fundamental elements to understanding self-will. The first is what you would consider important factors in your life.

The second is about what are the important factors are in your life. When we started this process, our thoughts made us believe we are broken people who are not worthy of anything or anyone. This is simply not true… We are talented individuals seeking a blissful existence without the threat of violence in everyday life. Our needs and wants should be met and achieved, just like anyone else. Due to this fact, we become determined to gain the rights we deserve, sometimes at any cost. The price can be extreme when we are living in an abusive relationship.

When we finally chose to leave our abusive situation, we realized that we were not infallible. We made mistakes and had to look at our role in those decisions. Even though we are not responsible for the abuse portion of the relationship, we are responsible for our co-dependency.

This is defined in the dictionary as "codependency is a psychological condition or relationship in which a person is controlled or manipulated by another who is affected with a pathological condition (typically narcissism or drug addiction); and in broader terms, it refers to the dependence on the needs of, or control of, another. It also often involves placing a lower priority on one's own needs, while being excessively preoccupied with the needs of others."

- Codependency can occur in any type of relationship, including family, work, friendship, and also romantic, peer, or community relationships.
- Codependency may also be characterized by denial, low self-esteem, excessive compliance, or control patterns.

Narcissists are considered natural magnets for the codependent. When we function on our self-will and not live by God's will, we become confused and make mistakes, such as the ones listed above.

The realization of our character imperfections can be alarming and may cause us to deny those aspects of our character. They are; however, a reality, and we need to accept the facts to achieve complete restoration. The truth will set you free from the stronghold these negative emotions have on you. Self-will is not a bad thing; it is a powerful mental force when used properly.

To understand the *will* of God, we must first comprehend the concept of giving. *Will* is the giving up of something and the acceptance of something else. In this case, it's the promise of a new life free from the clutches of abuse.

The *will* of God is for every human to live in the comforts of love. If we doubt a bright, joyous future for ourselves, then that is what we will have: doubt. It is the only outcome we can expect when our minds stay clouded with fear and uncertainty.

Accepting the consequences of our actions is something we all want to ignore. Nevertheless, when we choose this path, it blocks all chances of conscious contact with our Higher Power, and learning to live by His *will* is impossible.

The passage of restoration shows progress with our faith in every area of life. We cannot pick and choose the areas we want restoration and the ones we don't. To progress with our chosen freedom, we must surrender to the *will* of God and trust that he will protect us in the future. Releasing faith is the common denominator between peace, confusion, and unjustified acts of insanity.

Based on the outcome of each phase, we have learned forgiveness, surrender, acceptance, and finally the importance of communication. Preserving a conscious contact with our Higher Power is the only way to achieve the success we desire.

Mind Power Four Love:

"Just as the heart equalizes the flow in the body, so love harmonizes the thoughts of the mind, bringing peace to both mind and body."

The next several phases are designed for the exploration of our character, and we learn to identify the exact nature of our wrongs. During the next section, you may find that your problems existed long before the abusive relationship started, maybe even as a child.

    The mechanics of working through this phase will require an uncompromising inventory of past actions. Some memories conjured from listing your moral inventory may be disheartening and even painful, but the process can lead to the relief of pain, guilt, and shame. As long as you continue to carry the painful memories inside, restoration will be difficult.

If you have apprehensions about beginning this phase, it may be helpful to expel any misgivings or reservations about the difficulty of discussing the past. Turn your attention instead to the positive aspects and benefits of working through this phase. Then keep an open mind to what may be revealed..... Remember, the information disclosed is for your eyes only. This is a safe place, no one is here to judge you.

As a young child, depending on your upbringing, the concept of moral and personal values may have been foreign. Nevertheless, they are imperative to success. Belief is having faith in a particular area of your life. In other words, what you value the most creates the environment in which you live. Whether it's money, sex, career, clothes, drugs, or power matters. You must decide what's important.

If your morals are based on solid spiritual principles, your life will be a success. If you dwell on the toxic memories, your life will follow suit.

Many of us have some type of morals or an idea of what values are, no matter how misconstrued they may be. The basic definition of morals is based on what somebody's conscience suggests is right or wrong. So, with this knowledge, your morals will change with whatever you focus on the most and consider important. In this case, working through these phases will help you establish a moral code based on spiritual principles.

An Inventory of Ourselves

This portion is designed to help us understand how the decisions we made affected our life. This phase is not about other people, it's about us. Writing about the experiences with other people is necessary, but you must only look at your part in the situation.

Some of us have struggled to find fault in our part of the abuse. Rest your mind now; you are in no way responsible for the abuse, although the decision to become involved in the relationship is another story. This is the reason for Phase Four; it teaches us how to look at our part of any situation. The underlying factor is based on behavioral patterns. When you start to create a moral inventory of your life, the patterns develop a well-laid-out map. The process compiles experiences in your past and puts them on paper. In doing so, it will bring clarity to the situation. It stops our minds from denying areas of the past that cause us pain. Consider this survival mode in its finest glory.

The mind power of love is not only about acknowledging our behavioral patterns, but about acknowledging the resentments we carry around. We can have resentments about anything that has to do with human society. Any emotion based on a feeling of being wronged or a sense of being treated badly is resentment. We list these items to shed light on the reality of the experience or how we viewed the situation. Our outlook on the experience is important to the restoration process.

Since old resentments have festered the longest, it's best to start with them first. Recognizing the past sheds light on the present because they can manifest themselves in various ways. After listing all the resentments, you will begin to identify behavioral patterns, which are the clues you need to proceed with the restoration process. The outline breaks down each little piece of the puzzle. You may be surprised to discover the vast majority of these patterns are learned behaviors from the past. We are all products of our environment, whether we choose to be or not. The good thing is we don't have to stay products of the past; we can initiate the life we choose at any time. The actions we establish by working through these phases will create a solid foundation to be successful.

As we complete each phase, especially this one, some unfamiliar feelings may surface. Through the process of formulating an inventory, our healing process began to break up the hardened surface we have kept for survival. By expelling these negative emotions, it allows us to shine, exposing the wonderful passions we carry for life and helping others.

The ability to examine our feelings in this section is similar to the way we analyzed our resentments. So many of us have buried our feelings so deep, we may not even know what it is to feel joy, peace, and freedom. You may have had brief moments of these feelings, but most of the time they were predicated on when the sensation was going to stop! In a sense, those instances were filled with intense terror, while we waited for the mood of the situation to change. Times such as these are the reason we bury our feelings, and rediscovering them can lead to additional trauma. However, the release will bring healing and emotional stability.

When we hold unspent hostility and anger, it slowly eats away at us in ways we don't even realize. It stops us from enjoying the wondrous miracle of life. We stayed wrapped up in a cocoon filled with fear and doubt, afraid of our own shadow. The miraculous events that can happen in our lives are far better than anything imaginable, but we must take the first step. It's time to stop letting the abuse rent space in your head…

It is estimated that 70 percent of all disease is caused by suppressed emotion. Regret, sorrow, and remorse tear down the cells in the body. So, if these thoughts are not neutralized, they can create a deadly poison that causes sickness and sorrow. Our thoughts generate actions, so use mind power to create beneficial healing in the body. Just as the heart equalizes the life flow of the body, love harmonizes thoughts of the mind.

Activating the mind power of love requires daily concentration to produce a positive love current. In return, these thoughts will break up and dissolve opposing thoughts of hate, guilt, shame, and humiliation.

When we were forced to survive in a situation filled with possessive limitations, it constricted our sense of freedom. This restriction brought feelings of shame and humiliation, along with the guilt we carried over thoughts of escaping our abuser at any cost. Sometimes, the results entailed bodily harm to our abuser, adding additional remorse. These feelings are normal survival impulses that result from an abusive situation. You should not feel guilt over wanting to stay alive or free from harm.

A substantial portion of the abusive relationship involved sexual encounters that were both consensual and forced. Sexual intercourse is a personal act, which is meant to be based on love and respect for the other person. When the sex turns cruel and abusive, our very nature is violated, and we retreat even further within ourselves. The withdrawal is so severe that sometimes it's like we have another person living inside, and both are fighting for control. These are all normal emotions after a traumatic event, and your participation is nothing you should feel shame or guilt over.

If discussing sex in any context is uncomfortable, you are not alone. But talking about your sexual encounters could help. However, this is not something to rush into, so take all the time necessary. Cataloging the sexual encounters of the past is a reminder of our imperfections, especially if the incidences relate to abuse from molestation, threats, or being forced physically. Humans learn through repetition and observation. In other words, we are products of our environment. You must learn to be at peace with your sexuality. It will be the deciding factor for future healthy relationships.

Abuse

We must use extreme caution before working on this section. You may even have to postpone this portion until a late date; use your judgment. If any doubts arise, write them down for discussion with a qualified professional. The pain you may feel inside by working through this phase can be unsettling. In most cases, someone caused these incidents we trusted or believed loved us and admitting we were violated in any way can be troublesome.

It is important to complete this phase but when you are ready. However, the secrecy of carrying this pain inside can cause continued destructive behavior. By confessing the truth of our abuse, releases the pain and allows our mind and body to heal. Abuse is never acceptable in any circumstance. We are not to blame.

If discussing the situation with another person is too painful, write the experiences in a journal. Be honest with yourself, once you are done burn the diary…. flush the feelings out of your system.

Assets

Many of us have spent a good portion of our lives focused on mistakes, or being reminded of weaknesses. When we only identify with the nature of our wrongs, it can amplify the misgivings. This vantage point leaves us a one-sided picture. Our lives have been filled with enough pain and anguish. When we learn to build good character traits it develops our assets.

We are all creations of the universe, and each one of us is unique and crucial to the fabric of life. Your presence on this planet is important. The phases of this program will help you discover your true purpose.

One method of finding success is to write out your plan, from beginning to end. The more specific you are about the achievements you want to attain, the greater your success will be. Another ingredient is to think big, and don't put limits on your abilities. With God, all things are possible. This portion is fun, so take advantage of the time, by objectively detailing your dreams and goals with good intentions. It will provide the success you desire.

Begin this section with two actual success lists. The first one should be a timeline detailing your restoration process. The second will be the list of your plans, dreams, and goals. Start with simple goals that you can build in each day; doable accomplishments. It is meant to boost self-esteem, not diminish it. Don't forget to include past success. Be proud of your accomplishments.

Create a timeline for your success.

    a. Be specific.
    b. Don't fear success.
    c. Think big, dream big.

Keep Your Goals for Success to Yourself

"When Someone Can't See Success for Themselves They Can't See It for You."

At this point in the program, many of us feel unorganized even disoriented. The message behind this step is very revealing and should be contemplated before continuing.

If you are feeling this way, you are not alone. Many of us have discovered secrets we just cannot reveal to anyone. In this case, write the account on paper, listing the details. After this, account for all the aspects of the incidence and burn the paper. Release it to your Higher Power and let it rest; don't give the issue another thought. Remember, you can never hope for a better past. Let trust and faith be your guide.

Revelations of this magnitude can create many false misgivings. It is suggested that you might want to discuss the findings with a qualified professional. The past can creep up at any moment and provide false information. So, having a second opinion is always a great confirmation. Exploration of these emotions is important, just don't dwell on them for too long.

Mind Power Five Power:

"Every word brings forth after its kind - first in mind, then in body, and eventually the affairs of the individual."

By admitting to God, ourselves, and another person the embarrassment and humiliation we feel for the violence that retained our life, we engage in the stages of restoration. Our admittance encourages trust in the restoration process. We can only live with the hope of restoration if the desire to achieve success is greater than the desire to remain in our current situation.

Our mind and body are connected as one unit. When abuse happens over time, the ramifications become reality. So, these traumatic situations create an adverse reaction with all parts of the body. The mind begins to create reasons for the abuse, as it compensates for the confusion, pain, and anguish caused by the situation. Without any new information, the mind uses past experiences to produce these ideas. In this case, the circle of violence continues in a repeating pattern until something causes a drastic change in reality. The alteration breaks the unyielding cycle of devastation, and a new transformation begins.

When we chose to seek freedom, it was likely because something in us died. Change can only occur after the death of something else. It is the nature of the universe. The desire for change is the perpetual creation of life itself. Therefore, we must generate words, thoughts, and actions with the fullness of life.

Our body feeds on words, therefore when those words are life-giving, they are health-producing. Words cause the atoms in your body to vibrate and change place — first the mind, then in the body, and later in your affairs. Your conversations can create ill health instead of good health because of the wrong words. The words you speak closely relate to the heart's true nature. Therefore, admitting to God and another person the true nature of your pain releases all negative toxins within the body and mind. It is then that restoration is possible.

In our abusive situation, the idea of forgiveness was not the center of attention, our survival was. Most of the time, it became apparent that change was necessary for life to continue. However, finding a way to escape and getting out alive did not seem possible until we opened our minds to release. It was the concept of change and hope that instigated an escape plan. Once these seeds were planted and the growth began, we were able to see a way out. The distraction was an ideal outlet, as it gave us a reprieve from the abuse. Hope was alive again, and freedom became a reality. However, the thought of admitting the humiliation of our abuse can bring feelings of terror. We fear the ramifications of societal recourse, rejection, or additional humiliation. What we don't understand is admittance alone can bring us the peace we so desperately need. Once we gain the courage to talk openly with someone about our past, we realize they are not so different.

As survivors, we lived for extended periods without any contact with the outside world. We could go for days, weeks, even months without a single conversation with another person. The talks we might have had were supervised by our abuser and/or closely regulated as to the content of our dialogue.

We had little time to be alone, and even simple trips to the grocery store were supervised. Someone else completely planned our life, from the clothes we wore to the food we ate, and who our friends would be. We became prisoners without being incarcerated.

Fear became the stronghold over our lives in every facet and learning to let go of the one thing that helped keep us alive causes terror in itself. This is compounded by the fact that the admittance of this humiliation to another person can seem unbearable. But you are not alone, and restoration from the abuse is possible.

When we take the first phases of freedom it's intimidating and may be overwhelming, but remember you have already survived the ugliness of abuse. Determination alone is an accomplishment of the utmost importance.

In this phase, we must focus on being honest with ourselves and commitment to the truth. It is an essential part of healing. We cannot grow by remaining in denial.

Practicing self-honesty is an essential part of the restoration process and is the only way to find true happiness and freedom. These realizations are painful. However, if we channel our attention to other feelings that emerge through this process, we can wake up to the promise of HOPE.

Mind Power Six
Imagination:

> "The imagination is the scissors of the mind; you create the pictures, which take your thoughts and give them form."

We begin working through Phase Six, filled with relief and an idea of what freedom means. Our hope for a future without abuse is bright. We've seen the damage from our past and how it affected the present -- a glimpse of how we can begin to correct the issues. But first, we must be willing to have God remove our character imperfections.

In the process of working through the last five phases, we have started to discover the patterns in our behavior and learned how we are likely to act on the same imperfections over and over again. This awareness brings a conscious acknowledgment of our actions and the willingness to remove our imperfections of character. These imperfections are a creation of the past we endured. They do not make up the person we are inside. Our true nature is the total of our thoughts. The image you carry on the inside is what shines through for everyone to see. Patience and continual work are the keys to consistency and the only pattern that initiates complete restoration.

While we struggle through these phases and work on the new life we desire, the process can seem like a lifetime, especially when we face terrifying images and thoughts. Sometimes, it creates a false reality that leads us to believe we cannot survive on our own. This is false, an entirely ridiculous concept. The fear is what keeps us locked in this train of thought and minimizes our patterns of behavior. Unfounded fear remains long after the real situation has passed. Only by accepting our character imperfections and understanding why they have controlled our lives; can we begin the release and move forward.

The concept of understanding a character imperfection may appear unnatural or confusing. However, some of us don't feel we have any imperfections and are just fine as we are… this is false reasoning. As examples:

- Do you carry negativity toward yourself or someone else?
- Do you manipulate others for your gain?
- Do you have dishonest intentions?

We must learn to control our thoughts and images, thereby keeping them geared toward restoration. Maintaining an avenue of continued growth is imperative to your personal development. The conscious effort we make is necessary to achieve change.

Vision

Science has proven 20 times more nerves are running from the eyes than from the ears. Results come much quicker when you picture what you want over hearing or being told by someone else. Clarity is the key; picture the images as already in place. In other words, if you want to be healthy, imagine yourself youthful and vibrant. Practice this technique for a short time every day, especially when you start to feel depressed or unsure about your situation. Change comes when you are willing to embrace the future as bright and prosperous.

1. How many times have you wondered what your life would be like without the abuse and constant life-threatening torture?

The process of wanting things to be better and live safe, free from harm is normal. A life filled with comfort and prosperity is a promised part of believing in a Higher Power.

Along with faith comes the power of release. When we ask for release from the problems that plague our soul, we are given the tools to achieve the result, providing you do the work. "Faith without work is dead."

It is the technique we use to create the release that counts. Just as working through the phase requires consistency, so does faith and your conscious contact with God.

Improving your connection with the God of your understanding is a process based on personal beliefs and knowledge of a Supreme Being. The sense of your Higher Power will become clearer through working on Phase Six.

Our process for removing character imperfections in this phase is much like the first two. The only difference, we now have a clear idea of what acceptance and surrender mean. When we faced an abusive individual, the concept of control was out of the question. When our lives are surrounded by controlling people, it will eventually lead to the elimination of the person we were meant to become. We learn to suppress any emotion that could cause an outburst of another abusive situation. This state of mind allows our survival instinct to run at full force. In doing so, our body becomes so accustomed to this flight or fight response, reality no longer exists in our lives. We become detached from our bodies. Our minds become separate entities, and as the abuse continues, we completely cloud all emotions. We must learn during this phase to unlock that vault, become vulnerable, and ask these imperfections to be released.

The List

Character imperfections are indicators of our basic nature. These natural behaviors make us human. In these actions, we make the same choices as others; the decisions are based on needs, wants, and sometimes desires. It is how we act on these emotions that force future events. When we learn to maintain balance and consistency through the guidance of our Higher Power, our lives become manageable. Our goal is to raise awareness of our imperfections so that we can become entirely ready for their release. This is not done by analyzing their origin or indulging self-degradation. It is learning to accept the choices we made and stop hoping for a better past.

List each weakness, and give a brief description. Then list the combating spiritual principles with their explanation.

Phase Six is based on the willingness to change our thoughts about who we think we are. In doing so, we allow the true nature of our soul to be exposed. Committing to the restoration process is a continual pledge to the life we choose to live, not the life someone picks for us.

The application of Phase Six is simply the willingness to accept the person we are, no matter what we think our character imperfections may be. It is imperative to love yourself just the way you were created; that includes your mistakes and achievements. Any unwillingness to accept the past and acknowledge the future as bright and joyful will eventually paralyze our spiritual growth.

The willingness corresponds with the faith you have developed by working through these phases. We must learn to believe that our Higher Power will work in our lives to the exact degree necessary.

As you progress in the restoration process, your life will change dramatically. It does not mean problems will disappear, nor will feelings of uncertainty about the future. The emotions may even seem overwhelming at times. But during these times, the most growth can be achieved with the right frame of mind. It is the act of learning to dream and create the life of our choice that many never imagined possible. Therefore, take this time to focus on the vision of what we choose to obtain in our restoration, and maintain this frame of mind during the rest of the process.

Mind Power Seven
Understanding:

"Understanding: Realizing past experiences can only harm my future when they are left unattended."

The phases were designed to strip away the past, along with the aspects of your behavior and actions that led you to this outlet. As the parts of our life are peeled away, it raises awareness of each shortcoming and allows us to better understand the choices we made and why the results turned out as they did.

The understanding brings familiarity and even a serene calm because we finally realize the consequences of the choices we made. As this process takes place, we appreciate humility and surrender. We anxiously desire to be released from the dark images of the past and focus on spiritual principles. As this process takes place, we also gain a greater understanding of our faith.

Our ability to comprehend the abuse and the role we played is crucial to our restoration. Granted, we are not to blame for the violence or destructive situation, but our choice regarding the initial relationship and partner is an area of our life we need to address. Studying the nature of our shortcomings is much like the work we did in Phase Six with our character imperfections. The difference here is that we can truly acknowledge the concept of acceptance. By humbly asking for this release, we unconsciously begin to remove character flaws.

Phase Seven may give us our first experience of feeling compassion for ourselves. We can make mistakes, forget something, or fail to complete all our daily tasks, and not fear an abusive situation. It's alright to just take care of ourselves.

- We can say no to something simply because it does not suit our needs.

- We can finally develop a connection with others, knowing that we are all subject to the same insecurities and failings.

- We learn to accept that our dreams and goals for the future are important.

- We are entitled to happiness, success, and prosperity.

To remove anything in our lives, we must be willing to walk away, no matter what the consequences are. The giving of something simply means making room for your greater good.

Once you learn to develop an honest, sincere relationship with yourself, it will grant an opening for the release of any shortcomings that are limiting your continual progress. When you can completely accept all aspects of who you are, your life will change in ways you cannot even imagine. These things include physical aspects, educational status, or financial situation, etc. Learning to center thoughts on your attributes and natural talents will allow you to become the incredible individual you were created to be.

Taking Action

At this point, you may wonder how you are supposed to feel. This is an important question because it will ultimately lead to the restoration. Our resolutions are key aspects to solving problems. You do not see with your eyes as much as you see through your eyes according to what you understand. The will to take action, according to what you understand, will move you to the next phase of restoration.

Since the human mind sees images, we gain knowledge and understanding through those images. Therefore, as you navigate the past, keep your mind open and search for the positive lessons that can be gained from those situations. Preparation for the outcome and how you visualize the future depends on how well you deal with the past.

You may find yourself feeling unsettled and struggling with certain aspects of restoration, even your spirituality. It simply means you are becoming aware of your behavior related to those actions. In most cases, these experiences are clear signs of success and the continual desire to better ourselves.

Our realizations of understanding the past create the path for an extended future free from abuse. Through these confessions, we create the knowledge to expand our future. The humble action of asking for the removal of our shortcomings is the predecessor to achieving the restoration you desire.

Mind Power Eight Will:

"Depend on the power of belief."

We have come to probably the most challenging section, phase eight. The task of making amends with our abuser --- dealing with forgiveness.

The ability to forgive someone who has caused us pain, sadness, or bodily harm - intentional or unintentional - is one of the most problematic aspects of restoration. The harm inflicted was both physical and emotional. However, the mental can supersede the physical in many ways. The wounds and bruises heal, but the scars are left behind. These emotions are far deeper than we can imagine in some cases.

The concept of forgiveness is an act of complete renewal, washing away the hurt, and unveiling the new. It is a spiritual principle that should not be taken lightly. There should never be fear in forgiveness because it allows the release of old memories and their experiences. When you have been washed clean from the past, your divine plan can unfold as intended. The quicker you release and forgive, the sooner your greater good can be exposed.

You may feel that reviewing or writing about the abuse will cause you more pain, but it is the opposite. By clearing the actual abuse portion, it allows the pain, anger, guilt, and humiliation to release. This leaves your mind free to accept forgiveness.

Many people think forgiveness is for the other person….. it is not. The only person hurt by carrying the extra weight is you… "What you resist, persists."

From time to time, you may feel waves of doubt or bitterness, and this is expected. You have been through a traumatic situation, and healing takes time, so give yourself a break. In this case, your reservations are valued. It is an important step that requires complete surrender for forgivingness to be possible. Forgiving is not something you just say, it's about how you feel.

Certain situations may require complete separation from our abusers. So, we not only face the anger of being abused, but also the anxiety of loss. It's not unlike the loss felt over the death of a loved one. Grief can also play a major role. Phase Eight will guide us through the steps of resolving our forgiveness issues.

Forgiveness Letters

The next task is called writing a forgiveness letter. It will be unlike any statement you'll ever make.

Your letter must be specific, entailing the details that encompass every hurtful word, the incidence of abuse, or the situation directed at you. The specific facts of the actions are not necessary, such as dates, times, duration, etc.

Begin writing this statement as if you were sitting across the table from your abuser. Explain why they hurt you, how it made you feel, and why you are angry. Be as honest as possible. Remember, this statement is for you, not them. Don't give them any more control over your life. Be angry..... but then let it go...

To begin this task, start with a list of names, the people who have hurt you in the past. It is best, to begin with, the ones who have harmed you the most, or are constantly on your mind. The people that you cannot seem to shake.

If some on the list are not abusers, that is alright, write about them anyway. Maybe you knew them in the past or even present, and they have left an everlasting impression on your soul. Good or bad, does not matter. The mystery must be solved before you can move forward.

This list is not only to make amends or seek forgiveness but also to search for behavior patterns and get to know more about the person you have been and want to become. Remember, this is about you, not anyone else.

Once the list has been written, it's time to get willing to write the forgiveness statements. These must be from the heart and sincere, otherwise you will continue to repeat the same patterns. Just promising ourselves we won't make the same mistakes again is not enough, because some behavior is so ingrained that we are not even aware of the effects it's had on our lives. Refusing to accept our faults is denial at its finest.

As you scrutinize the list, images of your past may surface. Some of these pictures may not be appealing, and many of them you've wanted to forget for a long time. By releasing these instances with love, you create forgiveness statements that come from the heart. Again, if anger fills your thoughts about these memories, then write it out. It is still coming from the heart. The belief you can find restoration on your terms allows the removal of these experiences.

The focus of honesty, courage, and willingness to work on this phase shows a true commitment to the life you have chosen to create. We must learn to forget about the resentments and not blame others for the choices we made. Stop accepting the past by justifying through excuses.

Our future is bright, filled with success, prosperity, and joy, but only if we are willing to let go of these resentments. When we bottle this negative stuff inside, it creates health problems and ruins every chance of ever having a healthy relationship with anyone. We will always be untrusting, spiteful, and leery of what might…. happen.

Anytime we can develop intimate relationships with other people it is what makes us grow. We can only keep what we have when we give it away. By maintaining resentments, we will continue to live a life of isolation, fear, distrust, and secrecy; the one thing we desired to flee. The choice is yours….

When we've stripped away all the distracting elements of our abuse and exposed the solid core of serenity, humility, and forgiveness, we are ready for the Ninth Phase. By sharing your feelings with another person, you will get a better insight into where your focus should be.

Mind Power Nine Order:

"Discern the difference between acknowledgment and acceptance."

The idea of being able to sit down and understand forgiveness is an incredible feat that should be celebrated. Due to the extent of our abuse, at one point the idea would have been out of the question. The point is that we come to a solution of mercy and compassion for another human being, even when they have wronged us.

As we begin the Ninth Phase it cannot be wrapped in a neat little package, or be disregarded as a minor phase, and accomplished quickly. This phase could take years to complete, or you may never fully finish it. When you are finally ready to write the forgiveness statements and focus on the outcome of each one, careful deliberation must occur to discern the consequences of that decision.

When we look at the decisions in our lives that created hurtful situations, the focus must be on the reasons our choice was made, not the abuse itself. Of all the phases, forgiveness takes the most discretion, because we must fully comprehend the past to move forward.

We all have different levels of abuse. Some may have been more physical than mental, while others contain extreme variations of each. Due to this deviation, the changes in your personality and disposition vary just as much. So, you may not even realize the transformations unless someone points them out. The next section of phase nine requires trust…. It's especially important to discuss any forgiveness statements with another person to help with clarity on our thinking process.

The changes in our behavior are usually so gradual we may not even notice. Therefore, it is helpful to have a guide in the process. Detailed journals are a great reference point.

The superficial guilt and shame seem relevant, but there may be underlying issues we are not even aware. Yet, sometimes we rush deciding to alleviate the pressure but in reality, it only compounds the problem. These issues could be the initial cause for the decisions we made to enter an abusive relationship. It is only after we understand the repetitive behavior that clarity is formed, and the real cause of our choices is unveiled. If we do not fully understand the message taught by working through Phase Nine, we will be venturing into another catastrophic situation again.

A difficult thing to achieve is limiting your expectations of a particular situation. By assuming an expected outcome, you diminish the true purpose of the experience. The key is opening your mind to only positive results. As you begin to call order in your life, everything will respond positively.

Establishing order is an emotional state of mind. First, you must be willing to stop the insanity, minimizing anything that does not resonate in a calm and orderly fashion. Stop making decisions based on someone else's suggestions, concerns, or forced control over your life. These lessons are part of the process and restoration of working through these phases. It's the awareness of choices you have to make that are important. Stop, look, listen, and then decide.

One of the most challenging amends you will ever make is to yourself. Therefore, it must be a priority; release will come only when you are at peace with yourself. We have struggled with fear, and have been manipulated by controlling behavior and rage. Even the consequences of our actions have brought us shame. In many cases, it seemed that no matter what we did, it was not right or enough. We were always wrong.

Then after an extended period, we began to believe these lies, causing us to doubt every part of our life. We took it so far as to justify the lies and excuses with plausible statements in certain situations, you may have even found yourself defending the abuser. The decision allowed them to blame you.

Anyone who manipulates your feelings for their benefit is a clear sign of a traumatic situation that could never end with a hopeful outcome. If you find yourself denying this statement, it's time to focus on the purpose of the Ninth Phase.

The sole intent of the Ninth Phase is to set right the damage of the past. In doing so, we grant ourselves freedom, restoration, and a balanced relationship with us. Just being okay with who we are and the choices we made.

If we can reach a point to be okay with the person, we see in the mirror, it's a major step in the restoration process. It is good to want more out of life; giving, receiving, and sharing.

As you progress through the Ninth Phase, you may have people on your list that you owe amends. If this is the case, the same process follows as amends made to you. Start with a letter of explanation concerning the exact nature of your wrongs. Keep in mind the purpose of this face-to-face encounter is not how the amends are received, or whether we receive amends in return for the harm done to us, it is about righting a wrong. We are not making the amends to coerce or manipulate a reciprocal acknowledgment.

Making Amends

Once the statements are written the process of preparing for amends is complete. If you are making amends in a face-to-face meeting with anyone, you may feel as though you could walk on cloud nine, due to the freedom from the guilt carried inside. Such a feeling could be a whole new experience for you and something to keep close to your heart. It is the first taste of freedom from the past.

The work you have done is paying off. If you go forth with this frame of mind when you make amends, the chances are greatly improved that your admission will be welcomed.

The actual process of making amends is not always comforting. Our fears and doubts can well and cause extreme worry or stress about the outcome or how we will be received. In this case, we must rely on our spiritual principles to guide us through the process and trust that the outcome will bring the highest good for everyone involved.

The essence of Phase Nine is being relieved of your guilt and shame. The concept of freedom has been a long-term goal. Our obsessive behavior that resulted from the abusive relationship is finally becoming clear, and we are now aware of the signs. The darkness in which we survived has passed, and the freedom of a new life has begun. We can now begin to live with a fullness of heart and hope for the future.

Mind Power Ten Zeal:

"A graceful, flexible attitude working within each person, manifesting as great compassion and love."

The first Nine Phases led you to dramatic changes in your life. Some of them may be beyond anything you ever expected. We were able to conclude that our choices were not always accurate or successful, but we survived the situation. This path may not always be easy and free from problems, but with the knowledge we've gained, our tool kit is full and we are well armed to diffuse a situation before disaster can strike. As noted, this guide is meant to be a starting point, not the final word on any of the phases.

Feeling Versus Action

To begin the essentials of a personal inventory, we must first understand its importance. To keep what we have at this point, we must continue to practice the spiritual principles we have learned. You must learn to become more intimate with who you are as a person. This can be done by assessing patterns of behavior and doing a personal inventory. We must maintain a continuous awareness of what we're feeling, thinking, and even more importantly, what we're doing.

For example, if someone asks us, "How are you doing?" and we respond, "I'm terrible", the response comes from how we feel, not what we are doing. However, this response can have several meanings. So, we must be honest with ourselves and others about the true nature of the response. A daily inventory will solve this problem. It allows us to act on a situation before it becomes critical. Now, we may not always stop or prevent every situation, but we can control our behavior and emotions before, during, and after the fact.

By learning character qualities, we can control our behavior. Thereby, minimizing the way we react to certain stimuli. Our response is learned behavior, habits are what keep us in the same patterns. A written account is a conscious awareness of our actions, which helps alter the behavior.

All people are born with the ability to know right and wrong. However, in certain situations, we may have been forced to do things against our will, knowing it was wrong. As an instinct for survival, we participated in the event anyway, and now feel great remorse in having done so. We were living in survival mode and were reduced to an animal level. Our survival was essential.

The process of whether to make amends takes time, as many of us struggle to figure out what we did wrong. The choice should not be rushed or forced. Learning to trust our feelings and rely on intuition takes practice. The process will likely take the rest of your life, and it is not something you will ever perfect. It is part of being human. However, there is an inner peace you will develop deep inside; it cannot be mistaken once you learn to acknowledge it. The practice and completion of Phase Ten will help develop this insight.

If you are truly stumped whether you have done or said something wrong and need to make amends to someone, there are several options:

1. Locate the person and simply acknowledge that you may have hurt their feelings and you are sorry.
2. Write about the experience and pray about the situation.
3. Discuss the problem with a trusted person to get advice.

The decision is personal, but ignoring the situation will only compound the emotional trauma.

Unlike the previous phases, we have now moved on to living in the present, not the past. It is our first impulse to make an excuse or deny the choice we made. This doesn't excuse our behavior, because we are reacting to a potential conflict that may not even exist. So, we must begin to acknowledge our actions and promptly assess our decisions. Apologizing for the choices we make in our lives is no longer necessary.

Taking My First Personal Inventory

The essence of changing any habit is consistency. Experts state it requires 31 days of constant acknowledgment and exercising the alteration to change behavior. It does not matter if the behavior is good or bad --- but you must be acutely aware of your daily actions. A journal will help progress the action of changing our habits.

Constant integrity with ourselves is imperative for continual restoration. In the advent of becoming whole, develops moral values that will withstand throughout your life.

In the tenth phase, we learn the importance of self-discipline, honesty, and integrity with ourselves and others. This practice takes consistency and commitment to the future and the life we choose to live. At no time can we ever hope for a better past. All we can do is attempt to avoid repeating patterns.

Along with working through the tenth phase, we have learned to admit our wrongs, and with such admittance comes freedom unlike most of us ever felt. Being whole is a state of mind that will eventually become something you desire. However, the lessons taught us we are not inferior but are equal to anyone else. Our life is important, and we play a crucial role in the fabric of humanity.

The last portion of this phase began to give us a glimpse of the future. We have the freedom to create any kind of life we choose -- success and prosperity rest solely on our actions.

Mind Power Eleven
Elimination:

"The power of elimination is constantly infusing more energy into one's being, and simultaneously casting out of mind and body all waste. The forgiving love of our Higher Power is not only a wonderful spiritual stimulation for the soul and body, it is an important factor in the elimination process. It causes an infusion of the new as letting go of the old takes place."

The Eleventh Phase is the search for inner enlightenment that develops a higher conscious contact with the God of your understanding. Along with this exploration, we will learn the concept of faith. The dedication will foster the means to your spirituality.

The conviction to seek spirituality is unique to every person. Only through prayer and guidance can we continue to grow, so whatever approach you choose, the process is personal and unique. Either way, the important factor here is that we continue the journey.

One aspect that is essential to healing is the law of forgiveness; it brings forth new life. When we surrender, it draws on the strength from God, the divine source. Therefore, old errors fall away, losing their grip on our lives. You must learn to accept the presence of new as the outworking of our restoration.

Praying and Meditation

One exercise that will develop a conscious contact with the God of our understanding is learning meditation or prayer.

The practice of prayer and/or meditation is as diverse as your spirituality. But the one basic model you need to form is a dialog. Relationships are a two-way street, and both parties must give to receive.

Prayer is talking to our Higher Power. It might not be through speech; it might be in our actions or the evolving feelings we carry. Either way, the communications must remain constant and progressive. Through the sequence of these phases, you have created a solid foundation to build on. Many of us have designated the process of prayer to specific times of the day, which helps develop good communication habits. These behaviors will also spill over into other areas, improving restoration in all aspects of your life.

If this is your first experience with working through the Eleventh Phase, it may be a surprise to know you have been praying and meditating during this entire process.

This process develops patterns of meditation. As stated before, meditation is as unique as the prayer process and spirituality. What you are learning are some guidelines for developing an understanding and knowledge of your Higher Power.

When you begin to meditate, try to minimize distractions, especially electronic devices, so you can concentrate on knowledge from your Higher Power. Our understanding of communication is not always a set of words or instructions; it may simply be a feeling or emotion. However, through regular prayer and meditation, it comes to us as a quiet sureness of our decisions and the lessening of the chaos that used to accompany our lives and thoughts.

In a pamphlet written by Myrtle Fillmore in 1866, she recalls how her life was guided by conscious contact with God.

She states, "Life is simply a form of energy, and has to be guided and directed in a man's body by his intelligence. How do we communicate with intelligence? By thinking and talking, of course. Then it flashed upon me that I might talk to live in every part of my body and have it do just what I wanted. I began to teach my body and got marvelous results."

As she projected the positive affirmations upon her body, the life energy began to grow and heal her illness and soul. After being diagnosed with tuberculosis and given six months to live, her body healed and she lived another 40 years. This is merely an example of what the human mind can do when focused.

There are so many ways people can have a conscious awareness of God, but it simply means we notice or feel a presence in our daily lives. Faith does not come and go or fade in and out. Our awareness is what comes and goes, according to our moods and deep feelings that constantly affect our conscious contact. This makes it imperative that we closely watch the attitude we have about ourselves and others. Learning to maintain a healthy relationship with our Higher Power helps minimize the negativity that flows throughout the day. Meditation is a powerful tool to combat negativity and doubt.

The whole intention of this journey is to help promote restoration. It is in the searching that we find conscious contact with our Higher Power. God's will brings an inner sense of peace that gradually spreads throughout the body, a sign that restoration is taking place. Once you have acknowledged this feeling, hold it close so you can recognize any variance in the future, to keep your life in balance.

The last portion of the Eleventh Phase is learning how to decipher your true purpose in life. It is something we have all sought after. However, what most of us never realize is that our true purpose is already active; we merely have to develop the skill to exercise it. Through constant prayer and meditation, the knowledge necessary to seek this information will be presented when the time is right. Only after you have found peace of mind, can you be ready for your true purpose.

There is a saying: "more will be revealed." This concept is based on living by the will of God, not yours.

Our practices in this phase show up in every area of our lives. As we continue to practice the principles, balance will be established, our sense of urgency will be released, and we become secure in the process. Restoration is a journey, not a marathon.

We can finally become content with who we are, and satisfied with the life we have worked to achieve. Our focus can gradually switch to being of service to others, extending the gift of hope to them.

Chapter Six:

Confidence for Life

"There is more to sex appeal than just measurements. I don't need a bedroom to prove my womanliness. I can convey just as much sex appeal, picking apples off a tree or standing in the rain," Audrey Hepburn

What Is Confidence?

Confidence is best described as a belief in your abilities. It means you must find balance between too much and not enough. When someone appears too confident, they can come off arrogant, even snobby. If you lack confidence, it portrays unsureness, or people may think you are untrustworthy. When either state of being is too high or low, it can cause someone to stumble on unforeseen obstacles. Projecting the perfect amount of confidence helps gain credibility and develop a long-lasting impression. It allows us to deal with the personal and professional challenges head-on.

Many people who have tried to develop confidence may have come up short in their findings. But why? Confidence is something that must be developed, partly as a learning experience but mostly as maturity settles in. It is a tricky process.

Let's try an experiment, think back to a time when you tried to do something, anything that came easy? You did not have to think about it, it just came easy…… For example, are you good at communication, do you feel comfortable in crowds, can you build things, are you technically inclined, and last but not least, do you calculate mathematics in your head?

Take some time with this test…. how do you feel when amid the situation?

Discovering these things is one of the most worthwhile pursuits of your life.

Now Let's Discuss What is Sexy?

Ladies when you see a HOT man! What do you find attractive?

List items below:

_____
_____
_____
_____
_____
_____

If any of those items were the bad boy image, his money, clothing, or appeal that is not the true meaning of sexy, or confidence.

Below is a list of what it means to be sexy:

1. Confident
2. Caring
3. Well-groomed
4. Stylish clothing with class
5. Health-conscious

6. Motivated
7. Stable legal job
8. Genuineness

Confidence seems to be the one thing most people find extremely attractive. But what is it about confidence that makes it so sexy? Why are we more likely to be drawn to someone confident than to someone insecure or needy?

The one appealing trait of confidence is being noticeable, not afraid to take risks to enhance their life. There is a certain air about them that draws you in, but only if it makes you feel powerful. You want to know what makes them so self-assured. They're intriguing and we're beguiled.

Confident people can push us to be better, without a negative sentiment in their suggestions. Nor are they afraid to express themselves. Apparently, this is quite a turn-on in the bedroom. They say. Not me — I'm staying out of this one.

One other trait is of high importance, confident people don't be something they are not, they are happy in their skin. It is a matter of honesty, following through on a commitment.

But…. if it still confuses you, let's explore the other side of the equation. When someone lacks confidence, they are insecure; apprehensive, and anxious. Are you always in a hurry? Do you worry constantly about things out of your control? Do you call people to question them about a decision you made?

When you act in this fashion, it takes a great deal of energy and mental stamina. Strength that can one day cause major health problems. But that is for another time. Do find this behavior attractive in someone else? We have all had those kinds of friends that you wince when their name shows up on the Caller ID…..

On a personal note, there is something primitive and alluring about confident people. There must be a subconscious need as humans to find people we can connect with on a conscious level.

Psychology Today says, "A second aspect of confidence is *certainty*. The more confident you are about a particular outcome, the surer you are that the outcome will happen."

Think about that for a moment. Do you want a surgeon to be certain about his abilities?

Now that you understand what it means to be sexy through confidence, let's talk about how to build confidence.

Below are some suggestions:

1. Get this done

   - Confidence is built on accomplishment.
   - Start with small goals and work up to the big ones
   - Set an alternative plan each day to achieve one goal

2. Monitor Progress

   - Keep a daily log (your accomplishments)

3. Do the Right Thing

   - Create a value system

     - Character definition
     - Your actions each day (are you proud of them)
     - How do you envision yourself?
     - Are you proud of your achievements?

- Do you want to tell everyone about what you have completed?

4. Exercise

    - Improves memory
    - Prevents depression
    - Increase health
    - Makes you look Good…….

5. Be fearless

    - Failing is not your enemy…..
    - Can't never did anything
    - Dream big…..
    - Let nothing stop you from achieving your goals

6. Stand-up for Yourself

    - Logically you think, "How can I be right when this person and all these doubts in my head are telling me I can't do this? Stop….. yes you can…. . And you have to tell those people, especially the voices in your head, that they're wrong. You have it in you, so tell them you believe in your goal, you believe in yourself, so you're going to accomplish it.

7. Follow Through

    - Do what you say you are going to do, period…..

- Actions speak louder than words

8. Think Long term

    - Think about today's goals
    - Plan for a year's accomplishment

9. What Others Think Does Not Matter

    - Be your person
    - Ask advice from positive, confident people
    - Keep long-term goals to yourself, they don't need to be announced to the world

10. Do What Makes You Happy

    - What makes you happy? Do it!
        - Always make time for yourself
        - Change your habits

In conclusion, if you want to be sexy, confident, find something that drives your passion. Procure the plan and research ways to achieve the obstacle. Self-confidence is not shallow. It's a deep sense of self-awareness within that builds confidence without the clothes or modern-day armor we love to cover ourselves in. Everyone has some measure of a lack of self-confidence, but it's how we handle the issue that matters. We need to get to a place where we are truly confident in ourselves with no coverings.

Mind Power Twelve Life:

"To affirm 'life' will make the life force flow throughout the body."

The last phase of this book is essential to maintaining freedom. Mind Power Twelve is based on Life. So, if you are reading this sentence, then you have had a spiritual awakening. The nature of the awakening is unique for each person... regardless of the past.

    The awareness of a higher power is something many people struggle with at first. But once the awakening emerges, individuals notice changes in their feelings. A spark will be ignited, allowing them to feel their purpose. Almost instantly, people will notice the growth. We still acknowledge accounts of the past and the importance of remembering them, but these experiences do not depict who we are anymore. Most of us feel we have a second chance at a new life. If you are still confused by the explanation, look at the small things….. sleeping at night, a feeling of peace, or thinking of the future.

The journey for us was not quick, but the painstaking effort we made transformed us into the joyous, vibrant people we are today. We look in the mirror and like the person we see. Recalling the past and looking at the way we lived is unthinkable.

Life has new meaning now, it's no longer something we just do. We remember that the expression of life is infinite. Dare to believe in the limitless possibilities for your future. Do not let inactive ideas clog your mind; rather, open your thinking to the awareness of a new life filled with creative ideas expressed through your affirmations.

Repeat this often: *"My mind, body, and affairs are now filled and thrilled with rejuvenating life."*

This one simple affirmation can transform your mind, body, and affairs, bringing alive the natural energy already present in your body.

These phases are a foundation to help us restart life on solid footing; a concrete slab that we create for ourselves through honesty, integrity, and determination. Our ability to endure the experiences over and over again, while working through these phases, allowed us to see that we have the power and strength to survive any situation.

We may be looking back at this point and remembering friends, family, co-workers, whoever, wondering why they did not survive in the abuse. The thought is sad, and we may even feel angry, but through this spiritual awakening, we learn to accept that our Higher Power has a better plan for us and them. We have to acknowledge they are in a better place, free from further abuse.

The message of restoration can be broken down simply: *"Live free from abuse, restoration is possible, and there is hope."*

Practicing These Principles Daily

When we talk about the principles of restoration, the key is "practice." These lessons cannot be achieved overnight. We need to actively pursue the lessons daily. The spiritual benefits we derive from working through these phases depend on the effort you apply.

The effective practice of managing our affairs is not specific; we cannot separate careers, relationships, or other areas of our life. Spiritual principles must be maintained in everything you do and everywhere you go. Integrity makes us who we are and what we stand for in life. Consistent prayer and meditation will help keep these boundary lines clear.

1. What are some areas in which I can practice the principles?
2. When do I find it hard to practice the principles?

3. What am I doing to rectify the situation?
4. Do you act appropriately and resolve any issues immediately, or do you keep the trauma inside, locking it away? The answer should be clear.

Setting Boundaries

One essential part of restoration is practicing unconditional love for yourself. No one needs love without conditions more than a Survivor.

By practicing the principles of unconditional love, it does not require that we allow ourselves to be abused. Sometimes the best way to help someone is to stop enabling them and pray for their restoration.

We join society with excitement; the simplest little things seem easy. Our self-confidence brings poise when mingling with other people. Suddenly, our sights are set on living, not just surviving. If you wonder what's next, that is a positive attribute. Keep searching to find your answers. It is through this search that we discover the true meaning of our purpose.

You should feel proud of your accomplishment. The painstaking efforts of the work you achieved have opened the door for a second chance at life. Enjoy the freedom.

As we reflect on where we came from and what our restoration has brought into our lives, we can only find gratitude. Each one of us has something special to offer the world, and through this transformation, you have the ability and knowledge to pursue those interests with complete freedom. It's only with an attitude of confidence that we can achieve complete restoration.

How Will I Express My Gratitude Today?

Purposed Survivor Additional Books

- Getting Out Alive
- Survivor Basics
- Initial Beginnings
- 12 Step Guide to Restoration
- Get Hired – 30-day Guide to Finding a Job
- The Broken Angel
- IAM – A Guide to Self-Realization
- I'm Free – A Guide to Living Free

Follow us: @purposedsurvivor.com

www.ingramcontent.com/pod-product-compliance
Lightning Source LLC
Chambersburg PA
CBHW070951080526
44587CB00015B/2255